Squant
The Pilgrims

By Susan Washborn Buckley

Squanto was a Native American.
② He became the Pilgrims' good friend

Squanto helped the Pilgrims
grow corn.

(3)

He helped the Pilgrims find
places to fish.

He helped the Pilgrims find
herbs and berries.

(5)

He helped the Pilgrims meet other Native Americans.

He helped the Pilgrims celebrate
the first Thanksgiving.

The Pilgrims were thankful that
Squanto was their friend.